First published in 2022
By Hone

Typefaces
Univers, News Gothic
and Century Expanded.

ISBN 978-1-9999577-3-5

Brand is how we find each other

Adam Lumb

Contents

The real question about brand

This is a branding book with purpose. It's not about defining branding, or branding design. It's about helping you to think about branding in a way that will actually do what you need it to do.

What is it you want the brand to do?

This book was written in 2020 during the first year of the COVID-19 pandemic. There has never been a more pressing need for branding to help organisations survive and thrive, during and beyond the pandemic. The origins of this book pre-date the pandemic when I began to question the approaches that I, and others, had used for branding cultural organisations and products in the cultural and creative sector during the 21st century.

Most branding work doesn't add very much value to what an organisation does. This isn't good enough at any time, but especially in an economic downturn or period of societal change. The 21st century has seen two major economic downturns; the financial crisis of 2007–08 and the pandemic impact of 2020–21. We need branding to do better – to help cultural organisations not simply bounce back, but also adapt for a changing world. Having worked in many different roles in the cultural sector and considered brand from a number of perspectives, I wanted to look at brand afresh for my own sake and I hope this approach helps you with what you are trying to do. If at any point you find your own direction to go in, please do. I hope this book is a springboard for your work with your brand.

This book will make brand <u>useful</u> to you. It will reconnect your brand with your product or service – bringing your audience back to partake more often with less effort from you.

It will give you ways to frame the problems you face and to find good solutions that work. And it will give you step-by-step guides to help you achieve what you want to do.

Adam Lumb

Why traditional brand definitions don't help

In 2020, the world was struck by the Covid-19 pandemic. Museums, galleries and cultural venues that bring people together in physical spaces found themselves reeling, unable to connect with their audiences in traditional ways and unable to operate their visitor-facing commercial businesses, such as their shops and hospitality. Cinemas and theatres closed. Whilst some cultural products such as film and TV boomed on streaming services, film production was shut down or became increasing difficult and costly to make. Other publishers of print material (books, magazines and comics) were cut off from traditional retail distribution. There was a rush to move online – which only increased competition in the digital space.

Brands now need to be more effective than ever. I'm tired of branding work that isn't really effective.

You may consider that your brand is:

– **your logo**
– **your philosophy**
– **what you stand for**
– **your big idea**
– **why you do what you do**

These are all justifiable definitions, however these definitions focus on what it is rather than what its purpose is. When seen through the lens of "what is it you want to do?" there is another way to look at brand.

The story of the exhausted barrow boy

Once upon a time there was a barrow boy. He was poor but he worked hard every day. Each day he would trundle his barrow to the market with his goods to sell. One day he had green apples and he shouted about his wares until his voice was hoarse and he had sold all his apples. He trundled his cart home, tired but pleased to have sold all his apples.

The next day he had pears to sell and trundled back to the same spot in the market. They weren't so ripe as yesterday's apples. Some of his customers came by, but they weren't so pleased with what he had to offer. The pears weren't good and anyway, they wanted apples.

Across the market from him was a new stall. It stood out from all the others. It sold apples and other fruit. The stallholder wasn't shouting about her wares as loudly as the boy. But there was a queue. The boy didn't sell much, despite all his shouting and sales patter, and trundled home.

On the third day, the boy had apples to sell again. He trundled his barrow back to the market but someone was already in the spot he had yesterday. He shouted about his apples until his throat was raw, but hardly any of his apple-buying customers found him in the market throng.

The next day he had apples to sell at the market. They were good, ripe apples and he got his regular spot in the market. He sold a few to passers-by but some of his apple-buying customers from before did not visit him that day. His voice was almost gone from shouting about his wares. Across the market was the trader at the new stall. A queue had formed again, many of the same faces from the queue the other day.

As he sadly packed up that evening, having sold very little, he trundled his barrow past the new stall holder across-the-way as she was packing up.

"Why is it" said the boy, "that you have a queue and have sold more fruit than me every day when I am shouting so much louder than you about what I have?

The stallholder turned and looked at the boy and his barrow.

"It's not just about how loud you shout." said the stallholder. It's about making it easy for the people who like what you have to find you again and again. And don't worry about the ones who don't like what you have to sell".

"I sell stuff because I work harder than you," said the boy. "And that means shouting".

"No," said the stall holder sadly. "What you are doing is re-starting your business every day. No wonder you are tired."

Not branding is like restarting your business every day.

The story of the only blacksmith in the village

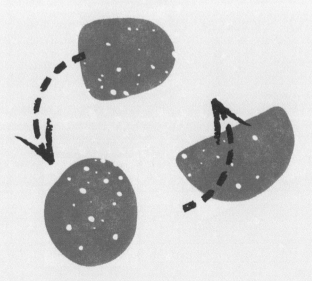

Far away in a small kingdom in a small village there was a blacksmith. He was the only blacksmith in the village and only he had the skills to smelt and hammer and make the repairs and new items the villagers needed. He didn't need a brand. If you didn't like what he offered, you couldn't get what you wanted. He was successful by his own definition.

As the blacksmith's family grew, he realised he needed to make more money and grow his business. So, one day, he travelled to the city in the hope of something more. He toured the blacksmiths' forges of the city. Some were less skilled than he, some were more skilled. Some specialised in repairs, some specialised in armour. Some sold to the aristocracy, others sold to farmers.

"How am I going to stand out against all of this?" he thought.

Brands serve a purpose <u>relative to the competition they face.</u>

And so, we come to the purpose of branding and the title of this book…

Brand is simply a way to find each other.

For you to find an audience...
...and for them to find you.

Introducing the Marketing Iceberg

Marketing is aligning what people want with what you have to offer. Marketing is a matching process. Brand is a tool that helps you find each other to complete the match.

Comms

Offer

Research

Aligned and matched

Marketing is often seen as a promotional activity. This isn't surprising, as that is the bit you can see. But like many things, it is the tip of the iceberg. I developed the iceberg model as a simple way of understanding what marketing is and how you can use it to improve your success rate.

Above the metaphorical waterline of our iceberg is the visible "communication".

Below the waterline is the "offer". This can be a product or service that solves a customer want or need.

And below that at the base of the iceberg is "research" to understand your audience's wants or needs. This means that communications, offer and research form your COR (core) or ROC (rock) solid foundation.

You can work this model starting with any aspect, but the important thing is to ensure that you are aligning the right offer to the audience that wants it, and communicating it in a way that clearly says it will solve their need or want.

So, for instance, you might start with a need and then solve that need. Or you might start with a product (for example a film or book) and then find an audience that aligns with it. Both work as long as they align. The primary difference is that if you start with your product or service, then your audience will only ever be as large as the audience that your product or service matches to (and will be constrained by the product's appeal).

Alternatively, if you choose to start with a target audience in mind, then your product's appeal will be constrained by the size of the audience.

Depending on the business that you're in, one approach may give you better results. As always, it comes down to **What is it you want to do?** Wherever you start, the important thing is to ensure that you align the three tiers of Communication, Offer and Research with each other.

Once you have that alignment, your brand will become the through line to keep things together and help you and your audience to find each other again and again.

Finding your place in the world

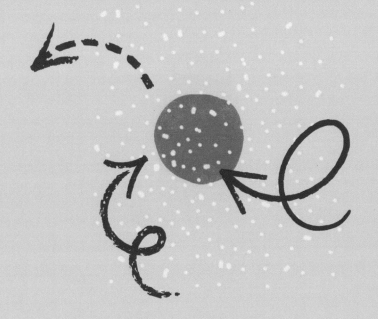

Can your audiences find you? Can you find them? We have so much choice as consumers. In the physical world, and especially in a digital world, we have more cultural product vying for attention than ever before. The challenge for businesses is being found. And some products and services on offer aren't really that different. A lot of products and services can do the same job as well as the next one. Some of the products and services that we need as consumers we don't regard as that important or worthy of much deliberation in our choosing. In essence, brand simply helps consumers find the product or service that they believe is right for them – whether the decision is simple and quick or a key decision.

So how does this help us...?

Because it shows us that we should stop getting lost in brand creation strategy. Instead, we can simply ask ourselves if we have matched the right product/service with the intended audience that wants it and if we have we helped audiences find it amongst our competitors?

For decades, organisations have written vision and mission statements (usually with confusion about which is which).

With the new approach outlined in this book, you can dispense with vision and mission statements and have one very simple document that will work to shape your brand for audiences and for your staff.

What follows is a step-by-step guide to finding your brand's place in the world.

Know your reason

Good brands know the reason they do what they do – and so do their audiences.

In order to unpack the **reason** that you do what you do, you should be able to answer the question "why do you do what you do?" with a simple sentence beginning "**because**…" Put simply, brands should be able to say why something is important with the addition of because…

"**Because**…" engenders action. **Reasons** polarise people too. Not everyone will like your answer. "**Because**" can be serious and lofty, or fun and playful. **Because** is a **reason** that can connect logically or (for a more powerful connection) emotionally.

Feelings are important and reflected in language such as:

> It's not my cup of tea.
> It's not my kind of place.
> I just don't fit in here.
> It's not for me.

Brands that can stimulate and match the emotional connection to their audience can sometimes maintain more loyalty, prevent product switching and create products and services less sensitive to changes in price.

An exercise to find your reason

To understand the reason that you do what you do, be "the three year old in the room". Keep asking "why?" and answer "because…" to peel back the layers until you can go no further. It can be very revealing to understand your reasons about what you, your organisation and your audiences really think and value.

If you founded the organisation, ask yourself the question. If your organisation is older, look at the reasons given by the founders. Are they still relevant today? Keep asking why you do what you do.

For example, perhaps you started your organisation and do what you do because you believe in being an ecological brand. Why is that important to you? Because without taking care of our planet we are all in danger? That's true of all brands. Why do you do it? Because you personally saw the harm being done to a particular region. And why did that matter to you? Because you saw how you could solve a particular problem? And why is that important to you…

Go as deep as you can and sometimes you will surprise yourself when you really understand why you and your organisation do what you do. However, beware. If you get to your reason and can answer with a **because,** also ask yourself "so what?". Your audience is thinking "so what?" too. That's okay. The best reason you can give for your brand won't appeal to everyone. It isn't supposed to and there will always be some people saying "so what?...". But the **reason** should compel action in you, your organisation and in your chosen audience.

Knowing and articulating the reason your organisation does what it does can be more compelling than traditional vision and mission statements. If your organisation isn't ready to drop them yet, knowing your **reason** will help you craft your vision and mission too.

Know what you offer

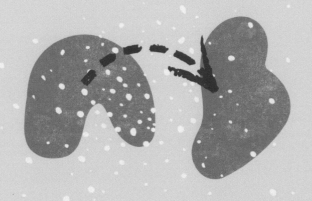

Thinking about the Marketing Iceberg model, what need do you actually fulfil?

Products and services must solve the customer need and do something functional. A car might have a <u>functional</u> benefit to get you from A to B. Even cultural products fulfil a functional need, and that function is often an emotional need. Film, theatre, art – all create emotion or stimulate thought in the audience, fulfilling an emotional or intellectual need. Or the need could be creating a space for people to meet and come together to socialise. Or to distract and escape from the real world for a bit. Or to learn. Or help people muse on certain issues.

You may have more than one offer if you are a large or complex organisation. That's ok. List them out.

Lumb's Brand Matrix

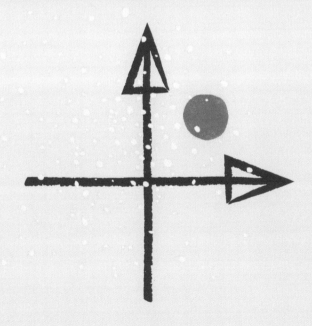

The job of successful brand creation is to help you and your audience find each other. This means that we need brands that:

i   match the audience to your **reason** for doing what you do

ii match the audience need to what you **offer**

iii ensure that these two reasons help audiences **find** your brand amongst other brand **competitors**

It's sometimes a struggle to separate the reason you do what you do from the purpose of what you actually do. And to help people find you and you find them I'd suggest that in fact you shouldn't separate them out as much as we historically have done in brand strategy. They are important in combination. Also, your brand is only relevant when considered against competitors, since its purpose is to help you find each other.

So, try this…

Lumb's Brand Matrix

How compelling the reason →

Compelling
Brands

Meh
Brands

Uniqueness of offer

Super Brands

Distinctive Product/Service Brands

$$\longrightarrow$$

All brands, including yours, will fall somewhere on this matrix. Along the horizontal axis from left to right we have the <u>uniqueness</u> of what you offer. This is the need or problem that your product or service solves. The further to the right-hand side your offer sits, the more unique it is (with the most extreme version being that you are the only product/service in the world who does what you do). Consider your unique selling points. Were you first to market, best or different to everyone else? Plot where your offer sits. Mark an "X" where you are located and next to the X add your brand's name and make a note of what your distinctive **offer** is.

Remember that this matrix is about where you sit relative to others, so consider where your competitors would also sit on this horizontal line. These are competitors whose **offer** is trying to solve the same sort of problem or need as you. Very few organisations will have no competitors trying to offer similar solutions. For example, if you are a publisher and your **offer** is books to entertain readers, then you won't be the only publisher fulfilling this need. Be honest with yourself about how unique your **offer** is. Map your competitors with an X, a note of their name and a note of their unique offer.

The vertical axis looks at how compelling the **reason** is behind what you do. Compelling brands compel action. For the people they resonate with (you, your colleagues and your audience) these brands make you want to take action. More about what makes compelling brands in the next section.

On the vertical axis, move directly up from where you plotted the **offer** and relocate your "X" and note about the offer. Next to your offer add what your **reason** is. Consider how compelling your reason is for your chosen audience to take action. The more compelling the reason the higher to place your brand on the vertical axis.

Repeat this process for the competitors you mapped, noting their offer and reason alongside their name and "X" mark. When considering how high to rank their reason consider how much it will compel the audience you are targeting.

Now simply look how far along the horizontal and vertical axis you and your competitor sit and this will place you and them somewhere in one of the four boxes.

The four boxes reveal some truths about brands and the branding industry.

The benefit of this model is that it allows you to consider where you are compared to your competitors and to take action to separate your brand from theirs, in order to help your audience find you.

Meh Brands

At the lower left-hand side, we have brands that don't have very unique offers, nor very compelling reasons to take action. I've called these Meh Brands because that's how they make people feel. If you find yourself here, don't worry yet. This is the shocking reality of branding. Most brands are simply labels that don't make you feel very much of anything towards them. These Meh Brands can still do the job of helping you and your audience to find each other. However, to increase how powerful your brand is, you can consider what to change in order to be in one of the other boxes, which will give you a greater advantage relative to competitors.

There are two ways to improve your distinction from other brands in the Meh Brand box.

Distinctive Product/Service Brand

You can continue along the horizontal access into the Distinctive Product/Service Brand box. Brands in this box may not have the most compelling idea, but their **offer** solves the audience's need in a way that is unique.

The aim at the most extreme end of the axis is to be the only brand to solve the problem in this way or to be the only brand to solve this problem at all. This is incredibly powerful and useful to your audience.

For example, IMAX cinema is a unique ratio, size and experience, different from other cinema formats.

Compelling Brands

Alternatively, moving up the vertical axis, the box labelled Compelling Brands does exactly that. The functional need solved by their offer may not be the most unique, but the reason they do it is so compelling to them and their audiences that people are compelled to take action. And in taking action, audiences will choose products from Compelling Brands over other competitor products that do the same thing.

Super Brands

Finally, brands in the final box I've termed Super Brands. There aren't many of them, because getting into this box is hard. To be a Super Brand your offer has to solve the audience's need in a unique way that your competitor can't, or you have to be the only brand to solve this need. And, in addition, your audience also has to find your reason for doing what you do more compelling than the reason your competitors do what they do.

This model declutters all of the unnecessary aspects of branding and allows you to see where you sit relative to competitors on the two most important axes for you and your audiences to find each other. What problem or need you solve for them and the reason you do it. Together. Mapped in one place.

Using the marketing Ps

But how do you then apply this thinking so you and your audience can find each other? To apply the ideas you captured on the brand matrix, you need to consider every aspect of your business. To do this you can use the well-established approach of the "Ps of marketing". For each of the areas below, consider what changes you need to make for the area to better reflect your brand.

People

Having everyone in your organisation on board with the brand is so important I've given it its own section later in this book. Having your people use the brand in the way I've set out will allow the rest of the areas to happen.

Promotion

Remember the **Marketing Iceberg** early in this book. Promotion uses communication. This is the top of the iceberg that everyone sees and it is important that you use your brand matrix to steer your communication ideas, content and approach. This includes creation of any logos and other parts of your identity. Once again, this is so important it has its own section later in the book.

Product

Once again, thinking back to the **Marketing Iceberg**, what you are **offering** your audience is key. Your product solves a need for your audience and this is captured on the matrix at the intersection of your **reason** and your distinctive **offer**. Ensure your products are in alignment with this matrix now and in the future, so you keep the promises that you make to audiences in your promotional communications.

Process

How you do things must be true to your brand matrix. For example, if your reason is environmental in nature then ensure you don't create processes which conflict with this. Everything must align.

Place

Where you do your work matters. Online. Offline. Local or global. Ensure that where you decide to do business doesn't conflict with your matrix.

Physical Evidence

Whether your organisation is working with audiences digitally or physically, consider how the fit-out of your buildings, your website and your packaging reflects your brand matrix.

Price

Does your pricing strategy reflect your brand matrix? If your reasons are all about access for all, then you can't price things so that only the most wealthy can afford what you do. Make sure your pricing approach aligns to the matrix.

Partnership

What does your choice of partners say about you? Using the example of an environmental organisational **reason**, you can't have suppliers or partners who damage the environment as it sends out a conflicting message to your audiences.

As you can see, your brand matrix will be embedded in every aspect of what you do. It is this consistency and alignment that will allow your audience not only to find you, but to find that your **reason** and **offer** are consistent in every element of their interaction with you.

What makes some brands more compelling than others

Love, fear, joy, loss

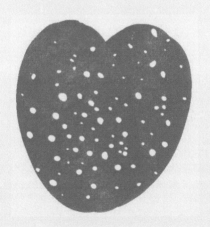

There's a difference between most brands and compelling brands. There are lots of brands that can sort of stand out from each other, but they aren't doing much to help people find them or connect strongly with the **reason** behind what they do. Some brands though are highly effective. Their **reason** for being is compelling for their target audience. Sometimes this is a large audience and sometimes it's a niche audience. But with compelling brands, audiences feel compelled to take action.

Compelling someone to take action requires a highly motivating **reason**.

As outlined previously in this book, your **reason** should be able to be articulated as **because**…

A look at some psychological motivations gives us some clues as to how to make our brand psychologically compelling. Compulsion is routed in our desire towards something or by our desire to avoid something. It's a basic pleasure or pain response.

Consider then the **reason** that you do what you do. Is it **because** you want to want to avoid something about the world or to change something about the world? Expressing your brand as avoiding a negative aspect about the world may create a tone to your brand that seems negative, however the field of psychology suggests that humans may avoid loss or pain even more than they pursue pleasure. If you would rather present your brand as a positive force, rather than avoiding a negative force, simply flip how you articulate your brand.
For example, if your brand reason is articulated as "**because** if we don't stop climate change, we'll run out of food" you may prefer instead to articulate the positive "**because** we are going to ensure we all have enough to eat tomorrow".

Compelling **reasons** speak to our emotions and/or intellect and are routed in human nature. Consider some of our core human emotions to help you tease out how your **reason** speaks to these concepts. This is not an exhaustive list, the **reason** for compelling action is as varied and complex as the human race.

- love
- status
- joy/happiness
- greed
- fear of loss
- guilt
- altruism
- need for approval/to belong
- curiosity
- sex

Brand as a solution to a risky business

The products and services of the cultural and creative sectors are different from those in other sectors. The brand matrix will work for all sectors, but with cultural sector brands there are some helpful things to consider when thinking through the matrix.

For example, cultural products are often unique. They aren't mass produced products that people consume every week, like tins of food. This is the reason that sequels and franchises of existing intellectual properties (IPs) are so popular for the film, TV and publishing industries. Without commenting on the quality of the art of any sequel, from a business perspective they make sense, as they are the next best thing to reselling the already popular original. This reduces the risk for both the brand and the audience.

In theatre, there is a long tradition of re-interpreting older works with new adaptations (Shakespeare, anyone?) as well as presenting new works. Remakes have become popular in Hollywood cinema too.

A similar approach is true for exhibitions for museums and galleries where existing "big name" artists or art works can reduce risks for new exhibitions. Reducing risk may not always create exciting new cultural product, but the attraction for businesses is understandable. Creating ongoing franchises of IP like this can mean that top writers, actors, artist/curators function as brands in their own right.

The challenge with the distinctive nature of cultural product is that it can be easy to think that it is a distinctive offer because no other offer can solve the need or scratch the itch that your offer does. And in a way that's true. However, whilst a thriller novel may be distinctive in and of itself, it sits in the genre of thriller where there are many others. To stand out it will either need to fulfil a more distinctive unique need or it really belongs in the Meh Brand category where it must fight alongside other books for recognition.

However, sitting above this turbulent cultural product, the brand of the organisation can unify these varied individual cultural product brands. If the audience identifies with the **reason** behind the cultural products and the organisation that produces it, it can even out the risk of all this varied content.

When applying this to the brand matrix, an individual cultural product would sit on the **offer** line. Genre is another label applied to help sort cultural product and it has more in common with the **uniqueness of the offer** than the **reason for the brand**. Therefore, genre will sit on the **offer** line of the matrix. In museums and galleries, subject matter might be used in place of genre in a similar way. This helps keep an understanding of the difference between the **offer** and the **reason**.

For example, the **reason** for the V&A's creation was, and still is, to inspire designers and artists. An exhibition on William Morris is "subject matter" and part of the **offer**.

Finally, when considering cultural product don't fall into the trap of thinking your competitors are only those who offer a similar product or service to you. If you are in the cultural sector you are competing for an audience's time. What itch do you really scratch for them? By understanding what need your **offer** really serves, you can ensure that the competitors you list really are your competitors.

For example, if you are a museum, you are competing not just with museums but with cafés, bookshops, cinemas and anywhere else people can come together and/or see culture. Depending on your collections and location, you could also be competing with other types of entertainment venues – so why would a family choose to visit you rather than a wildlife park or a leisure centre?

Asking your customers about how you help them is a good way to understand your **offer**, as is testing your **offer** and **reason** with them.

Remember though that they may not fully understand what need you solve for them. As Henry Ford allegedly said, "If I had asked people what they wanted, they would have said faster horses." Actually, people wanted to get from A to B faster.

So, thinking back to the **Marketing Iceberg**, remember that you can start with the audience's needs in order to define your **offer**. Or start with what you have created to **offer** to an audience. The point of the **Marketing Iceberg** is that you have to align your offer with what they want, whichever you start with.

The same is true of aligning the **reason** you do what you do with your audience, so they find it compelling. If the **reason** doesn't compel you and your colleagues though, it may feel false and you will struggle to make a genuine connection with your audiences or your colleagues. If you want your brand to move away from all the Meh Brands, seek out a **reason** you and your audiences really connect over.

Hierarchy and structure

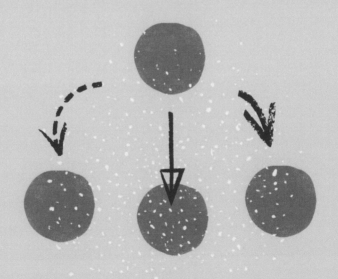

How is it that some brands can sell lots of different products and services that solve many different needs for many difference customers?

Many large organisations have multiple **Marketing Icebergs** – each aligning products and services to different audiences.

Disney is an interesting example with a range of companies to target all kinds of ages and types of people with its brands. Marvel would have a different iceberg to Pixar, as it is a different **offer** to a different audience.

The answers lie in brand hierarchy and structure options, known as brand architecture. The purpose of brand is to help us find each other and brand acts at the through-line to each **Marketing Iceberg**. Therefore, for each iceberg you may have a separate brand. This is known as an "individually branded approach" Many books and films may be released as stand-alone brands like this.

This is a highly effective way to ensure the matching process works and the intended customer finds the intended product.

The difficulty with this approach can be that it is expensive and potentially wasteful of energy and resource. Whilst it is very targeted, it does however require a lot of energy and money. This means that you need to consider whether the benefit of having lots of targeted brands outweighs the benefit of a broader organisational brand.

For this reason, some brands adopt what is often termed a "monolithic" approach where they focus all their energy on building a single brand.

To try to get the best of both worlds (organisational and individual product/service brands) many organisations adopt what's known as an "endorsed" brand model. In this model, the individual product or service brand is endorsed by the parent organisation brand. The volume control varies on this. Sometimes it is lightly endorsed in the small print. Sometimes heavily endorsed. In this way, the brand helps customers find not just one product they like but many products.

The advantage of both endorsed and monolithic organisational brands is that that they are extraordinarily efficient because all investment supports both the parent brand and the individual brand. The disadvantage is they aren't as targeted as an individually-branded approach.

To be effective across these multiple product, service or audience categories, the brand's **reason** for being must successfully compel audiences, regardless of the individual **offer**.

The reason must provide the common ground for all products and services it unifies.

Continuing the example of Disney and its acquisition of so many other brands (Lucas Film, Marvel, etc), Disney has to now see if its core brand of **Disney magic** can extend to these other brands or if they need to retain their own **reason**.

To plot an endorsed brand model on the brand matrix, the products/services must share the same (or similar) **reasons** for doing what they do. The answer "**because…**" **should be similar for both**. Look for commonalities in the reasons. If you can't make them fit, then you have two options. You may want to consider creating more than one organisational brand – each with their own brand **reason**. Or alternatively, consider whether an individually-branded approach would suit you better (in which case each branded product/service will have its own matrix). If you have some branded products or services that you simply need to force under your organisation's brand **reason**, then place them either under Meh Brands or Distinctive Offer. You can't force them to be Compelling Brands or Super Brands if they don't share the same **reason**.

The risk, of course, with an endorsed or monolithic model is that any negative reputational impact for one area affects the whole brand, just as any positive impact supports the whole brand. However, the benefits and efficiencies of whichever brand architecture you chose will help you compete with unbranded competitors and help you and your audiences find each other time and time again.

Lumb's Brand Matrix

Compelling Brands	Super Brands
Meh Brands	Distinctive Product/Service Brands

Uniqueness of offer

Why logos matter after all

Making your mark

Going back a stage, to the origin of the term "brand", it does actually mean a physical mark. (So, we can see why many people think branding is all about logos.) The "brand" is quite literally the burning hot brand used to brand cattle so that your cows were indelibly marked as being yours.

Of course, the "mark of ownership" has since been applied to other products and services over the years. An indelible link of belonging to a particular person or organisation, so you know what you are getting.

And this is where we can use the idea again of **brand as a way to find each other**. I mean it literally in the case of logos.

It is simply a way of bringing people together with what they want. It is there to help you **identify the one you want**.

So, the physical nature of the brand (logo, design, look and feel, sound and smells), isn't unimportant. You need to be able to distinguish it from similar things. And it also allows you to find something you like – preferably again and again, for both consumer and brand owner.

This isn't a book on logo design. There are lots of good ones. This is the place though to think about how to manifest your brand.

As well as helping you conceptually see your brand's place in the market covered earlier in this book, the brand matrix can also help you with how you present yourself to this market. Stick the logos of your competitors on it if you like. Choose key words and pictures to help you understand your brand and the brands of others. You now have everything you need on a single page. No lengthy brand personality tone of voice books. One page. Right there, with a constant reminder of where you are relative to competitors.

This can be incredibly useful to share with designers and creative staff when considering how you present yourself to the world, including the creation of your logo, because the matrix ensures you keep in mind that the purpose of brand is to help you be found amongst your competitors.

One of the most helpful pieces of advice I can give you when you come to work on manifesting your logo and working with designers and creative communications professionals is to think about how that logo sounds on the radio.

I highlight this to remind you that we humans have five senses and if you want people to use the brand to find you by how they feel, you need to consider all the senses. Don't simply focus on our visual bias. Thinking it though from all the senses will help you understand how to manifest your brand.

Brand as a filter for decision making

The world's perception of you is very public – especially in the modern age of social media. How you and your colleagues do things, and what you say in person and online, will affect how people feel about your brand.

Many leaders of organisations worry about how to manage these employee relations. They worry about employee brands and organisational development.

The reality is that, if managed well, "managing and leading through brand" becomes a freeing experience for everyone.

The key is to use the brand as a **filter for decision making**. The brand matrix can be used as a yes/no filter for progressing any idea.

A filter may seem restrictive, however, it is incredibly liberating as it moves all the decisions that need to be made away from the top of the organisation and distributes decision making across the organisation. Each member of the organisation "passes" the decision they are about to make through a mental filter and that filter is the brand's **reason**. They compare what they are planning to do with the organisation's reason for doing it. This is what "on-brand" means.

Command and control cultures cease to become as important. Staff are empowered. Every decision made that fits the brand's **reason** strengthens the brand. And, when applied to recruitment, it ensures that the team understands how they will fit in at the organisation and be happy there.

Having staff that share the **reason** for the organisation is far simpler and more powerful than mission, vision and value statements. Too many organisations focus on multiple elements, such as values in their brand and organisation development work, resulting in too many elements to be remembered. And this reveals the problems with this approach. Remembering a list of values is meaningless. Knowing lists of values for an organisation is not the same as sharing those values. Also, "official" values often end up being very similar at different organisations. Staff understanding the reason the organisation does what it does is simpler, creates genuine involvement and allows staff to bring their own values to being part of the organisation.

The caution with all brands is that, by virtue of the matching process, they are not for everyone. **They are for everyone matched to this particular brand – so that you can find each other**. This applies to staff as well as customers. And it's ok if a given brand is not for you, is not your cup of tea. Another brand will be. It's ok.

Adopting a branding approach brings benefits as a by-product of helping you and your audience to find each other.

The benefits are:

- a way of leading organisations and managing people
- a way to engage more people
- a way to make more money

Brand won't help you connect with all people. Just the ones who want to find you – and you to find them.

Summary

Brand is how we find each other.

It's a simple concept and I hope that by refocusing on the purpose of your brand you will be able to achieve better results for your organisation. Your brand sits at the intersection of how compelling the **reason** is that you do what you do and the distinctiveness of your **offer**. And it is this that will allow you to stand out from your competitors and be found by the people that want to find you.

Keep learning

This book is based on over 20 years of working to understand how brands work. I'm still learning though. We all are. So, I would love to hear from you about how the models and ideas in this book worked for you so I can continue to develop and make them better.

https://uk.linkedin.com/in/adamlumb

About the Author

Adam Lumb has worked in branding and arts marketing in the cultural and creative sector for over two decades. He has held positions in branding, marketing and commercial development at several cultural organisations and has worked across, theatre, galleries, museums, universities, publishing and television, including the National Portrait Gallery, London, the Royal Armouries and the BBC. He's held trustee and director roles on the boards for audience development agencies and the British Association of Picture Libraries and Agencies. Since 2012, he has also been working as an artist, writer and as an independent brand, marketing, and intellectual property consultant.

These templates of **Lumb's Brand Matrix** are provided for you to use in your own brand development as you work through the steps in this book.

Lumb's Brand Matrix

How compelling the reason

Uniqueness of offer

Lumb's Brand Matrix

How compelling the reason

Uniqueness of offer

Lumb's Brand Matrix

How compelling the reason

Uniqueness of offer

Notes

Notes